Quilted Postcards – The Flower Edition

'Little Quilts Of Creativity'

By Sarah Sparkes

www.tortoisecrafts.co.uk

Postcard design, text and artwork © 2021 Sarah Sparkes

Photography © 2021 Tony Sparkes

Editing Tony Sparkes

Proof reading Laura Sparkes

Published by Tortoise Crafts Publishing
All enquiries to: editor@tortoisecraftspublishing.co.uk

First Edition

First published 2021

ISBN: 978-1-8380342-1-4

Dedication

To the two people without whom this book would not get created. In many ways their names should be on the front cover with mine – my husband Tony who does all the photography and technical stuff to put the book together, and our daughter Laura who is my sounding board and takes my 'wordy stuff' and makes sense of it, minus a lot of exclamation marks!!

Thank you.

Sarah

Contents

Introduction

For years my husband and daughter had been telling me that I should share my Quilted Postcards with more people than those I send them to, or occasionally teach them to. One of my dreams was to create a book and, in 2020, that dream was fulfilled. 'Quilted Postcards Little Quilts of Creativity' was published. With a lot of work from both Tony, my husband and Laura, our daughter. It was a family project in what was a very difficult year.

I have made so many Quilted Postcards over the years that the 16 basic designs within that book were only the tip of the iceberg (or half of a box). So, I went through the other seven boxes I have collected over the past decade and found that I have lots of different 'themes' of postcards including flowers. We pulled out 15 for this book.

The flowers represented in this book are not meant to be perfect replicas of actual flowers. They do not look like photographs or drawn/painted artwork, they are representations in fabric, hopefully giving the feel of each of the flowers that I have chosen. Some are my favourite flowers, some are those that I have created for family and friends. I have tried to keep the designs as simple as possible.

Each postcard has been given a level of difficulty – easy, intermediate, and expert – to make it easier for you to work through them. I have also included a few extra bits you can make with the designs – bowl fillers and coasters.

What is a Quilted Postcard?

A Quilted Postcard is a 6"x4" piece of fabric art made using three layers. The size makes it a postcard and the three layers make it a mini quilt. They use the skills of patchwork & quilting and then add in some embroidery. Many of them are a combination of both, together making 'Little Quilts of Creativity'. They are perfect to be given as gifts to someone or to be mounted on a card and sent for special occasions. The limit really is your imagination and creativity.

I have included two other products in the variations that use the same techniques and skills, just in different sizes and ways of finishing. They give you more scope to be creative with what you make from my designs.

How to use this book

The first Postcard – Tulip – has detailed instructions needed to make the Quilted Postcards and I would recommend, if you haven't made one before, that you start there before making any of the other postcards in this book. The instructions for the other postcards only include instructions specific to that postcard. Throughout this book you will find , my logo. She marks where I give my personal hints and tips to help you make your postcards. I have also included a basic embroidery stitch guide and instructions to make bowl fillers and coasters at the back.

Happy Creating!

Sarah

Basic Supplies

These are the basic things that I use in making Quilted Postcards, bowl fillers, coasters, in fact most of the fabric based things I make! But remember you can use whatever you find works best for you.

Fabrics

As I am a patchwork quilter I have a huge range of 100% cotton fabric and it is these that I use for most of my Quilted Postcards. Cotton is easier to work and comes in a huge range of colours and patterns. For the back of the postcard I use a white cotton fabric. I buy a better quality bleached calico (USA muslin) for this.

Threads

I use a big range of threads on my Sewing Machine. I have lots of thread in my workroom and I use whichever works best with the current project. From standard sewing cotton, sew-all to rayons for embroidery and machine quilting threads. And plains to variegated threads. For the bobbin, however, I always use a white cotton. I have one in the machine and then a spare, filled and waiting to be used.

Stranded Embroidery Cotton

I use DMC, and as I also do cross stitch and so does my daughter Laura, we have boxes and boxes of threads. If you don't have any then I would recommend buying a few of the variegated ones, as they have light and dark colours in.

Iron on interfacing

I use Vlieseline H200 interfacing, as I find it firm enough to give the postcard the 'body' I want but not so thick that it makes it really tough on my hands for the hand embroidery. But use the product that you prefer, as long as it is white, and iron-on. Follow the manufacturers instructions for pressing the interfacing onto the fabric.

Wadding

All the wadding that I use is leftovers/offcuts from my patchwork quilting, as I prefer to use Hobbs Heirloom (80/20) for this, it is also used in the postcards. I would recommend a wadding that doesn't mind pressing, so not a polyester one.

Fusible Web

Use your favourite one – mine is Vlieseline Bondaweb, I buy a big box of it as I do go through a lot! Bondaweb is a paper-backed sheet of thin glue. Designs are marked on the paper side and cut out with an allowance all around. With the paper side facing up it is laid on the wrong side of the fabric being used and pressed into place using an iron to melt the glue onto the fabric. The shape is then cut out to the line, paper peeled off and placed glue side down onto the background fabric. It's then, again, pressed with an iron to melt the glue and attach the fabric to the background fabric ready to be stitched. Please follow the manufacturers recommended iron temperature for the fusible web you are using.

Sewing Machine

Although a sewing machine isn't essential for creating Quilted Postcards it does make them quicker and easier to do, especially finishing the edges. Every sewing machine is different, you know your machine best and the stitches it does and the best threads for it.

I use just three stitches to create the postcards, straight, zig zag and blanket (applique) stitch, but use what you prefer. I also prefer to use my walking foot (Even feed foot).

I would suggest that you have a bit of a 'play' with the setting on your machine, till you find the stitches and stitch width and length that you are happy with – remember to make a note of these settings. Sometimes if using a thicker thread you will need to change the settings, again make a note!

I guess I should tell you that I use Bernina sewing machines. The one that I use mostly is an Aurora 440qe. I also have two others – one I take to class (Activa 135) and my original 1130 that I bought over 35 years ago.

Crayons

Throughout this book many of the variations have added colour by using crayons. There are lots of crayons on the market but the one that I have found with the best and most even pigments and melts evenly into the fabric is Crayola Crayons. These are readily available in most craft shops and supermarkets. I recommend beginners to start with a smaller 24 pack – I have a very large box that a friend bought back from the USA for me.

When using crayons please remember to use a paper towel between the postcard and the iron so any excess pigment soaks into the paper towel rather covering the iron (Don't iron your husband's shirts with the same iron after this either!).

Marking Pencils and Pens

I use a normal pencil for a lot of the marking, please check that whichever pencil you use for drawing on the fusible web doesn't come off onto the iron, as it is really annoying to find that you have ruined a piece of fabric because the pencil has come off on to it! Especially a pale colour.

For marking on details to be embroidered I use Clover Air erasable pen and occasionally on white or very pale fabric a Frixion pen, but these tend to leave a white line on darker fabrics when pressed.

For writing on the back of the postcards and sometimes other bits I use a Pigma Micron Archival Ink black No.3.

Iron and Ironing Mat

Whatever you usually use. I have an iron and an ironing mat that is only used for patchwork because however careful you are accidents happen and fusible web or interfacing will get stuck to the iron or ironing mat.

Scissors

My preferred scissors are my Fiskars embroidery and Fiskars General purpose 16.5cm ones, these get used for everything!!! I know scissors should only be used for fabric, but I use these for fabric, fusible web and paper, I find them a nice size and weight.

Hand sewing needles, thimble, and pins

Whatever you find best and prefer.

Rotary Cutter, Matt and Rulers

If you have them then use them, if you haven't then scissors are as good. I have a big range of different sizes and makes of rulers. Use the ones that you are most comfortable with for the size of the project. I mostly, for postcard making, use my 6" square ruler and my 1"x14" one.

Odif 505 Temporary Adhesive spray

This is optional but I find it useful.

Starter Postcard—Tulip

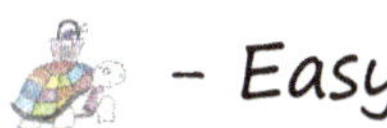 – Easy

I don't have to look far for inspiration for tulips in our house! I love tulips, I have a big bunch of wooden ones that we bought back from Amsterdam in a Denby jug on the windowsill, they make me smile every time I look at them. There are also smaller wooden ones around and a number of Quilted Postcards, Journal quilts and other bits with a tulip theme.

I would recommend that you make this Quilted Postcard first as it has the complete, full step-by-step instructions for how I create them.

You will need to make this postcard

2 pieces of white cotton fabric 4½" x 6½"

2 pieces of iron-on interfacing 4½" x 6½"

1 piece of wadding 4" x 6"

Fusible web

A selection of fabrics

A selection of sewing threads

1) Take the fabric for the background and draw a 4" x 6" (postcard size) rectangle onto the right side of the fabric cut out with a ¼" allowance all around.

Rather than constantly having to measure my postcard's backgrounds, I have a piece of card cut to 4" x 6". With this I can check a piece of fabric is big enough to make a postcard and also quickly mark the size, without having to measure.

2) Press one of the pieces of interfacing onto the wrong side of the background fabric.

3) Take your fusible web and place – paper side up – on top of the template. Trace on the design.

4) Cut out the traced design with a ¼" extra all round.

All my designs included in this book are hand drawn and so are a bit quirky, it's how I create patterns. They are also the correct size and way round for just putting fusible web on top and tracing the design straight on, without enlarging etc!

5) Take the fabric for the tulip and stem and press the fusible web pieces onto the wrong side of the chosen fabric with your iron.

6) Cut out the design pieces on the marked line.

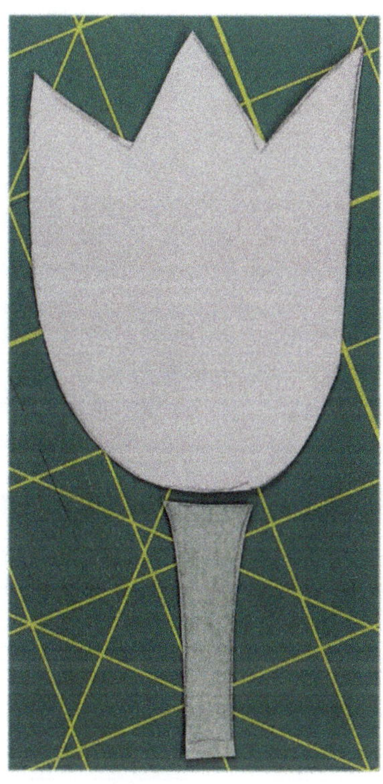

7) Peel off the backing paper and position in place on the background of the postcard. Press carefully in place with the iron.

8) Mark the petals on the tulip.

9) Layer with the wadding and a piece of white cotton fabric.

I use the 505 temporary spray adhesive to hold the layers together. If you are using this, please remember to spray it on the wadding and only in small amounts. If you don't want to use a temporary spray you can pin the layers together.

10) Using your preferred stitch and sewing thread, stitch round the petals on the tulip. Remember to pull the thread ends through to the back, knot together and trim off the ends.

I have used a narrow zig-zag stitch and a pink thread. I have gone darker with my thread. If I had matched the thread to the fabric, then the petals would not have shown up, so it is better to go either lighter or darker. On my sewing machine the size of the stitch is 0.4 x 2.4. I am aware not all machines can be adjusted like mine.

Pulling the threads to the back - this is really important to do, don't be tempted to just snip them off as they could unstitch, especially if blanket or straight stitch. I don't pull the thread from the back though, I start at the front, thread the ends through the needle (an easy threader needle is great for this!!) push the thread and needle through to the back, tie off and then cut off the ends.

11) Stitch the stem.

13) Stitch round the postcard, just inside the marked line, using zig-zag stitch. For the first round of stitching I use the standard setting on my machine, which is 1.5 x 3.3.

12) Take the other piece of white cotton fabric and press the other piece of interfacing onto the back. Pin this to the back of the postcard, making sure the white cotton is on the outside. This will make the back of the postcard.

14) If you are using a rotary cutter, ruler and mat, place your postcard on the mat – ruler along the marked line and cut off the excess fabric. Or you can just cut along the lines with scissors.

15) Zig-zag round the postcard again with a slightly closer and wider stitch.

 I use 0.9 x 3.6 for the second round.

16) Using a pair of scissors, trim off the 'fluffy' bits on the edges and also the ends of the threads.

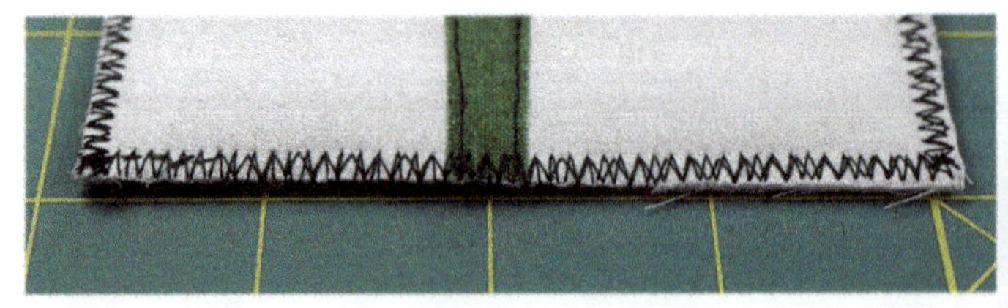

17) Stitch round the edge for a third time.

I use 0.5 x 4.0 for the third round.

18) Using a pair of scissors, trim off the 'fluffy' bits on the edges and also the ends of the threads.

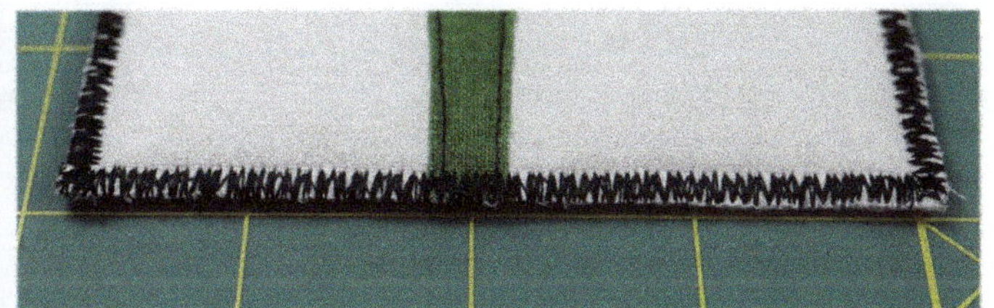

19) Stitch round the edge for a fourth time.

I use 0.4 x 4.2 for the final round.

20) Using a pair of scissors, trim off the 'fluffy' bits on the edges and also the ends of the threads.

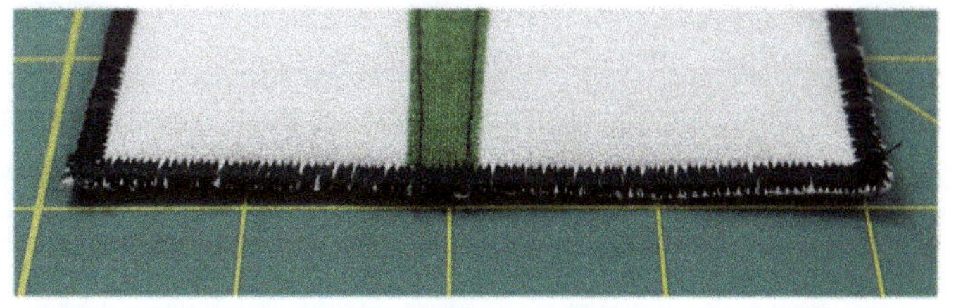

21) Turn to the back of the postcard and
    add any decoration that you wish.

For all my postcards I imitate a 'real' postcard. The centre line is drawn using a ruler and Pigma Micron pen. I then stamp my 'makers' mark underneath the centre line and create the postage stamp with a stamp of my logo – we have had both of these created in Rubber Stamps and I use a VersaCraft black ink pad. Using the Pigma Micon pen, I draw round my logo to create a postage stamp and then draw round a Gutermann 100m empty cotton reel to create the franking mark, the date is the date the postcard was made.

I have used a plain fabric and then coloured on details/ texture with Crayola crayons, and stitched round with straight stitch for both the pink and yellow versions.

For more about using crayons see the Crayon Flower later in the book

Smaller tulip postcard. It has a background square of 2" x 4½".

Bowl filler, finished size 3" square. The background is a 3½" square with the small tulip design appliqued onto the background.

Instructions for making the Bowl Fillers are at the back of the book.

Template for Tulip

Extra Template for Small Tulip

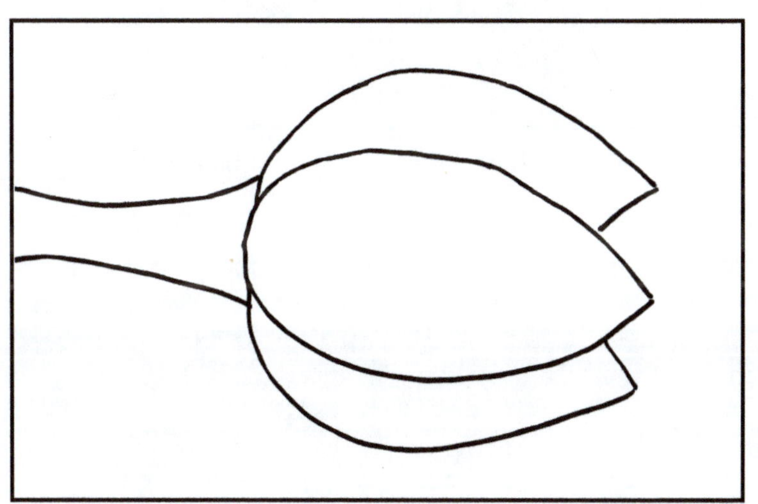

Allium

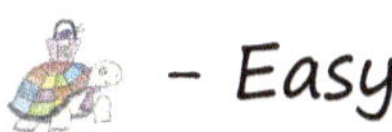 – Easy

Alliums are another of those flowers that I really like. I don't know whether it is the colour (my favourite colour is probably a purple, although the shade varies at times!!) or the shape, balls of small star shaped flowers. Whatever it is I really like them. I have tried to grow them in the garden but they never survive.

Behind where I teach is a historic garden and I enjoy walking round it to see what is growing. They have a fantastic bed of alliums and so I can watch them coming up, budding, flowering and even when they finish flowering they still look pretty.

You will need to make this postcard

2 pieces of white cotton fabric 4½" x 6½"

2 pieces of iron-on interfacing 4½" x 6½"

1 piece of wadding 4" x 6"

Fusible web

A selection of fabrics

A selection of threads

Stranded embroidery cotton – in purples or one variegated shade of purple

1) Draw the circle and stem onto the paper side of the fusible web and cut out with a ¼" extra all round.

2) Press onto the chosen fabrics and cut out on the line.

3) Press the design pieces onto the prepared background.

4) Layer with the wadding and rectangle of white fabric.

5)   Machine stitch the design.

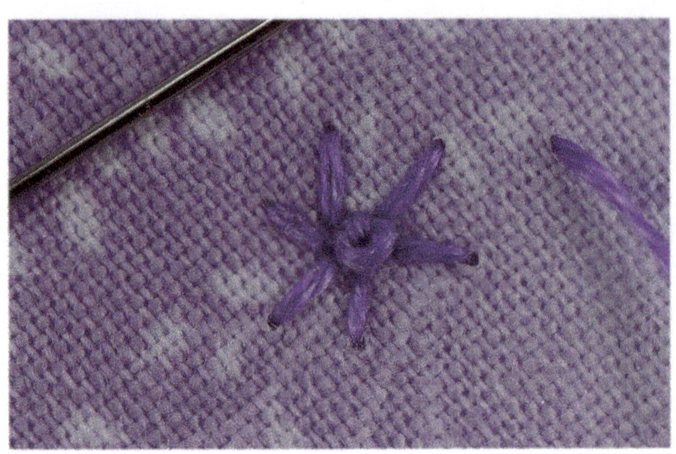

6)   Embroider the small star flowers by stitching a French knot and straight stitches coming out from the knot.

7)   Pin the stabilised white fabric rectangle on the back and stitch around a number of times till you are happy with the finish.

Bowl filler/mini cushion, finished size 3" square. The centre is a 2½" square piece of fabric with 1" wide strips for the border. The mini allium is appliqued on and then the flower and the stem embroidered.

This has been created by using five smaller circles in different shades of purple and embroidering each in a different shade of embroidery cotton.

This variation is using the bowl filler size template, put onto a 2½" square.

Allium's come in white as well as the lovely purple shades. This is my version of a white flower. I have tried making this in white material but it is too stark. So I have used a very pale green and embroidered in white to get the texture.

Templates for Allium

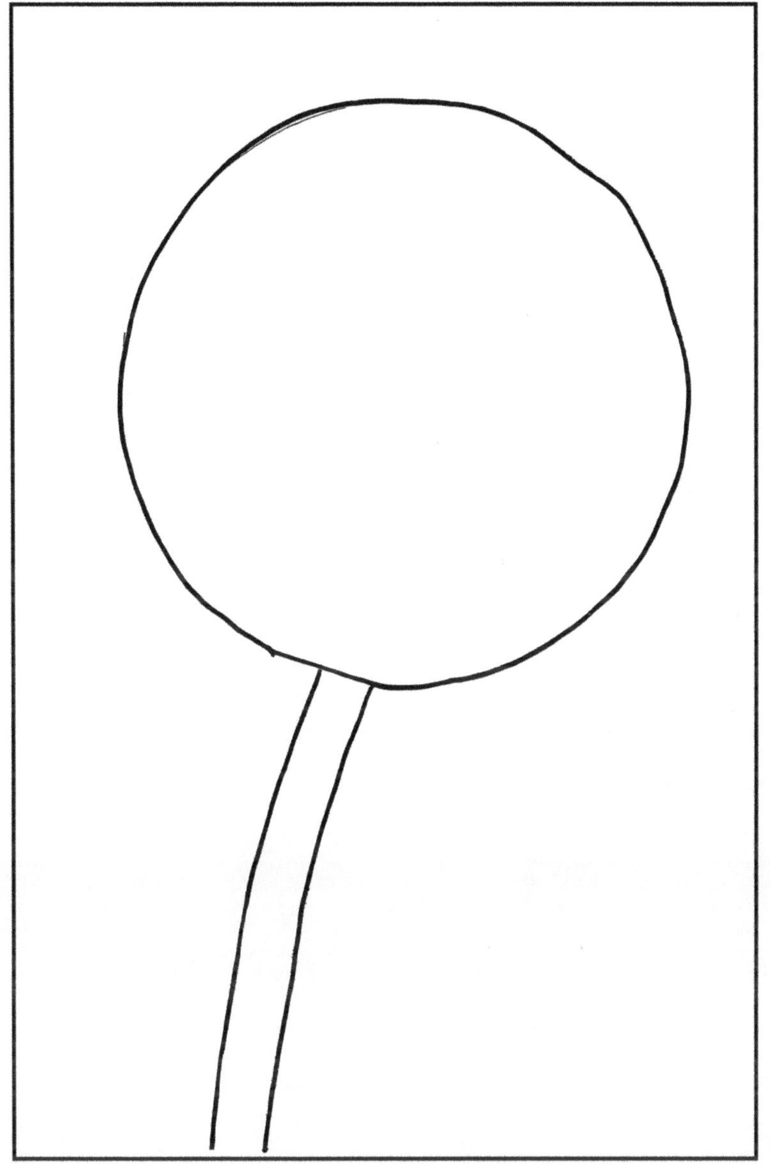

Extra
Templates for
Allium

Flappy Flower

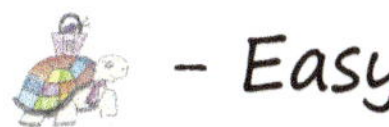 – Easy

I can't really remember what the inspiration was for this postcard, I think it was a pack of flowers and butterflies made in textured paper that Laura had to make cards with when she was very little!!

As for the name, I was trying to think of something to call this design and I asked Laura. She immediately said they are 'flappy flowers' and as neither of us could think of anything else to call them after that – it stuck!!! They are "Flappy" as the flowers (and butterflies on the variations) stand away from the background.

<table>
<tr><td>

You will need to make this postcard

</td><td>

2 pieces of white cotton fabric 4½" x 6½"

2 pieces of iron-on interfacing 4½" x 6½"

1 piece of wadding 4" x 6"

Fusible web

2" square of Iron-on interfacing

A selection of fabrics

A selection of threads

Stranded embroidery cotton - yellow

</td></tr>
</table>

1) Draw the leaves and the bigger flower onto the paper side of the fusible web, and cut out with a ¼" extra all round.

2) Press onto the chosen fabrics and cut out on the line.

3) Press the design pieces onto the prepared background.

4) Draw on the stems and details of the leaves.

5) Layer with the wadding and rectangle of white fabric.

6) Machine stitch the design.

7) For the smaller (flappy flower), draw the flower onto the 2" square of iron-on interfacing and then press this onto the chosen fabric. Cut out on the line.

8) Pin the small flower in the middle of the big flower.

9) Embroider, using French knots in the centre of the flower, through all the layers.

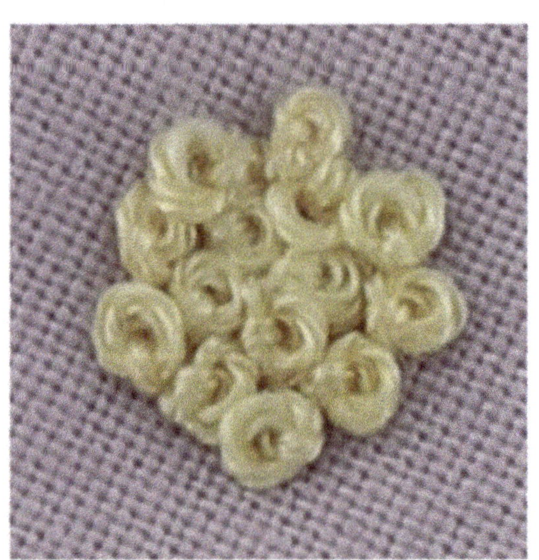

10) Pin the stabilised white fabric rectangle on the back and stitch around a number of times till you are happy with the finish.

This has a little more work to it. The background is created to look more like a paper card that has layers. The 3" square and ½" wide pieces are drawn onto the fusible web, then pressed onto the prepared background and stitched. The ground, snail, stems and leaves are embroidered, then the flowers and butterfly are attached.

This variation uses just the flower, with two butterflies all made to stand away from the card. The leaves and stems have been machine stitched but they can be hand embroidered.

Template for Flappy Flower

Extra Templates for Flappy Flower

Tulip Parade

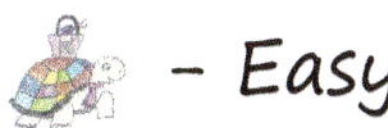 – Easy

The inspiration for these postcards is my love of tulips!!! And yes this is the second tulip postcard in this book! They are one of my favourite flowers, I plant galvanized steel buckets with them so I can look out of my kitchen window at them. I love the paintings/drawings and photographs of the plants as specimens and it is these that have inspired this postcard – a parade of specimen tulips.

You will need to make this postcard

2 pieces of white cotton fabric 4½" x 6½"

2 pieces of iron-on interfacing 4½" x 6½"

1 piece of wadding 4" x 6"

Fusible web

A selection of fabrics

A selection of threads

Green stranded embroidery cotton

1) Draw the leaves and flowers onto the paper side of the fusible web and cut out with ¼" extra all round.

2) Press onto the chosen fabrics and cut out on the line.

3) Press the design pieces onto the prepared background fabric.

4) Draw the stems, details of the petals, and a line ½" from the edge.

5) Layer with the wadding and rectangle of white fabric.

6) Machine stitch the design and round the marked line.

7) Embroider on the stems.

8) Pin the stabilised white fabric rectangle on the back and stitch around a number of times till you are happy with the finish.

Bowl filler, finished size 4"
x 4½". The background is
cut to 3" x 3½" with the
borders 1½" wide. A
single tulip is appliqued
and stitched on the
background.

A single tulip,
stitched with straight
stitch layered onto a
2½" x 3" rectangle.

Rather than stitch with blanket stitch I have used straight stitch on standard factory setting and a dark grey thread (Gutermann sew-all No.36). I find that black thread can look a bit harsh for this type of work and so I use a very dark grey as it is a bit softer.

Template for Tulip Parade

Viola

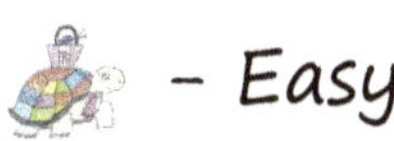 – Easy

To many there isn't much difference between a pansy and a viola, they are both the same shape but violas or wild pansies are really sweet. They have much smaller dainty flowers and aren't as big, bright and showy as the much larger cultivated pansies. I have a dark leaved, blue-purple flowered viola in my garden, it likes my shady garden and self-seeds all over the place, which I really don't mind as it is very sweet. Violas, as they are small, are very easy to overlook.

<table>
<tr><td>You will need to make this postcard</td><td>2 pieces of white cotton fabric 4½" x 6½"
2 pieces of iron-on interfacing 4½" x 6½"
1 piece of wadding 4" x 6"
Fusible web
A selection of fabrics
A selection of threads
Pigma Micron Pen</td></tr>
</table>

1) Draw the three sections of the flower, the 2½" square and the 1" x 4" strip onto the paper side of the fusible web and cut out with ¼" extra all round.

2) Press onto the chosen fabrics and cut out on the line.

The 'ribbon' strip doesn't go under the square, partly because it makes it very bulky and hard to sew through but also because if the 'ribbon' is a darker colour it can show through the square.

3) Cut the 1" x 4" strip in half to create two pieces 1" x 2" for the ribbon.

4) Press the design pieces onto the
    prepared background.

5) Layer with the wadding and rectangle
    of white fabric.

6) Machine stitch the design.

7) Draw the lines on the flower with the
    Pigma Micron Pen.

8) Pin the stabilised white fabric rectangle
    on the back and stitch around a
    number of times till you are happy with
    the finish.

Three violas on a pale green background.

Bowl filler, finished size 3" square. The centre is a 2½" square with 1" wide borders. A viola is appliqued on and then stitched.

I have gone for a waterfall effect, several viola are appliqued on and then stitched. I have used a very dark blue/purple thread.

Template for Viola

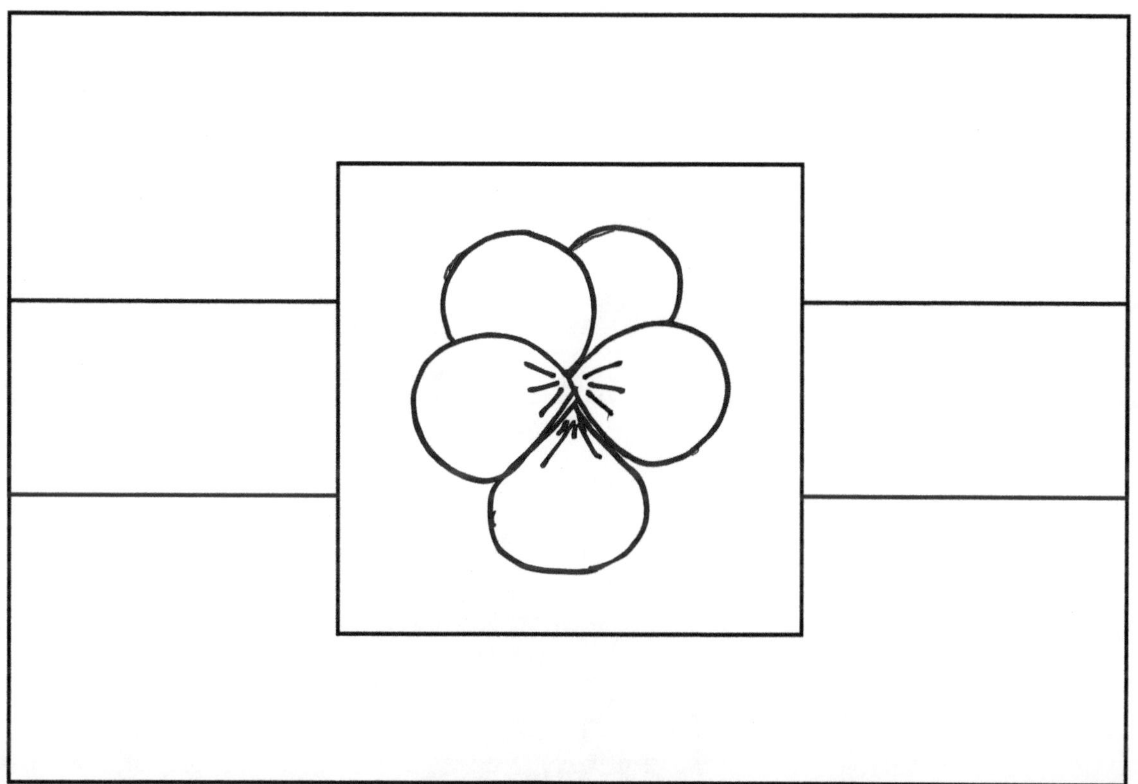

Extra Templates for Viola

Fuchsia

 – Intermediate

These are such delicate flowers, they are the ballerinas of the flower world!! And easily recognisable. I wouldn't say they are a favourite flower of mine, I have tried to grow them, but they just don't like my garden. They are a favourite of a couple of family members and friends and that why I have created them in fabric.

You will need to make this postcard

- 2 pieces of white cotton fabric 4½" x 6½"
- 2 pieces of iron-on interfacing 4½" x 6½"
- 1 piece of wadding 4" x 6"
- Fusible web
- A selection of fabrics
- A selection of threads

1) Draw the lower petals, the top petals, and the top onto the paper side of the fusible web and cut out with a ¼" extra all round.

2) Press onto the chosen fabrics and cut out on the line.

3) Press the design pieces onto the prepared background fabric.

4) Draw the petals and stamens on.

5) Layer with the wadding and rectangle of white fabric.

6) Machine stitch the design.

I have gone for straight stitch for this design, using the standard length on my machine with a very dark grey thread.

7) Pin the stabilised white fabric rectangle on the back and stitch around a number of times till you are happy with the finish.

I have created two
flowers, in similar
colours and used a
dark grey thread to
stitch both.

With this variation I
have used a softer
range of colours
and added a fabric
frame to the
postcard.

Template for Fuchsia

Collerette Dahlia

 – Intermediate

Dahlias are another one of those flowers I love, they come in so many colours, shapes and sizes, from small dainty flowers to huge bright showy pom poms. Individual plants are lovely but the best thing is a huge border filled with dahlias. At Anglesey Abbey in Cambridgeshire they have a big curving bed, backed by a hedge, that they plant with dahlias in a ribbon of colours, blending from one to the other.

There are so many different styles of dahlias, many are too complicated to create in fabric at this size, so I have chosen the simpler one of the Collerette Dahlia to create in fabric.

> **You will need to make this postcard**
>
> 2 pieces of white cotton fabric 4½" x 6½"
>
> 2 pieces of iron-on interfacing 4½" x 6½"
>
> 1 piece of wadding 4" x 6"
>
> Fusible web
>
> A selection of fabrics
>
> A selection of threads

1) Draw the inner petals and then the outer flower and centre circle onto the paper side of the fusible web and cut out with a ¼" extra all round.

2) Press onto the chosen fabrics and cut out on the line.

3) Press the design pieces onto the prepared background fabric.

4) Draw the petals onto the flower.

5) Layer with the wadding and rectangle of white fabric.

6) Machine stitch the design.

> I have used blanket stitch for the centre and then straight stitch for the inner small petals and finally blanket stitch for the outer petals.

7) Pin the stabilised white fabric rectangle on the back and stitch around a number of times till you are happy with the finish.

With the variation I have coloured the petals with crayon and then embroidered the centre with French knots.

2½" Mini Postcard. For this variation I have just used the centre of the Dahlia. Not sure it's very practical to send as a postcard!

A number of the designs in this book would work a 2½" minis as they have interesting centres.

Template for Collerette Dahlia

Rose

 – Intermediate

The inspiration for this rose was an embroidery transfer. When my Aunt died and we were clearing out her home, I came across a box full of embroidery transfers, some were really old loose sheets from magazines and others were in books. There were loads of them...... Roses, well white, blush and pale pink ones, are among my favourite flowers, I love the smell and the names I find fascinating!!! And the history and symbolism.

You will need to make this postcard

2 pieces of white cotton fabric 4½" x 6½"

2 pieces of iron-on interfacing 4½" x 6½"

1 piece of wadding 4" x 6"

Fusible web

A selection of fabrics

A selection of threads

1) Draw the leaves - six of them - and the rose onto the paper side of the fusible web and cut out with a ¼" extra all round.

2) Press onto the chosen fabrics and cut out on the line.

3) Press the design pieces onto the prepared background fabric.

4) Draw on the details of the rose and the stem.

5) Layer with the wadding and rectangle of white fabric.

6) Machine stitch the design.

7) Pin the stabilised white fabric rectangle on the back and stitch around a number of times till you are happy with the finish.

Instructions for making the Coaster are at the back of the book.

4" square Coaster using just the main flower and a variegated thread and zig zag stitch.

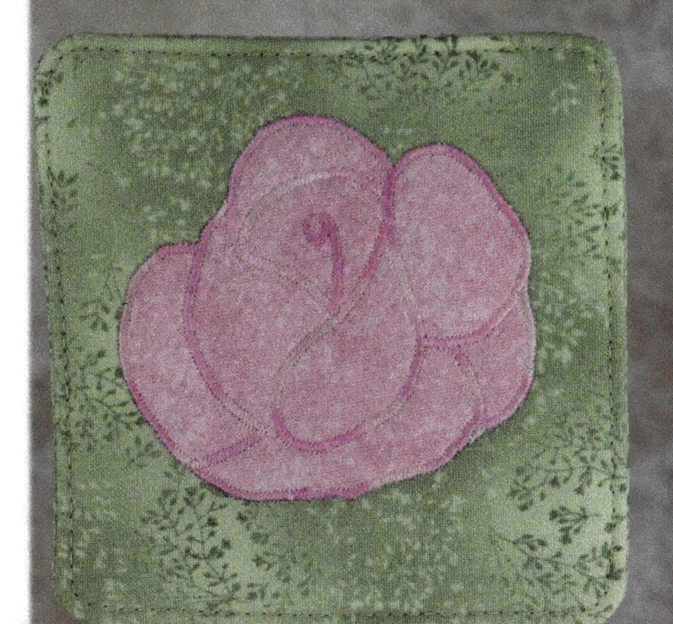

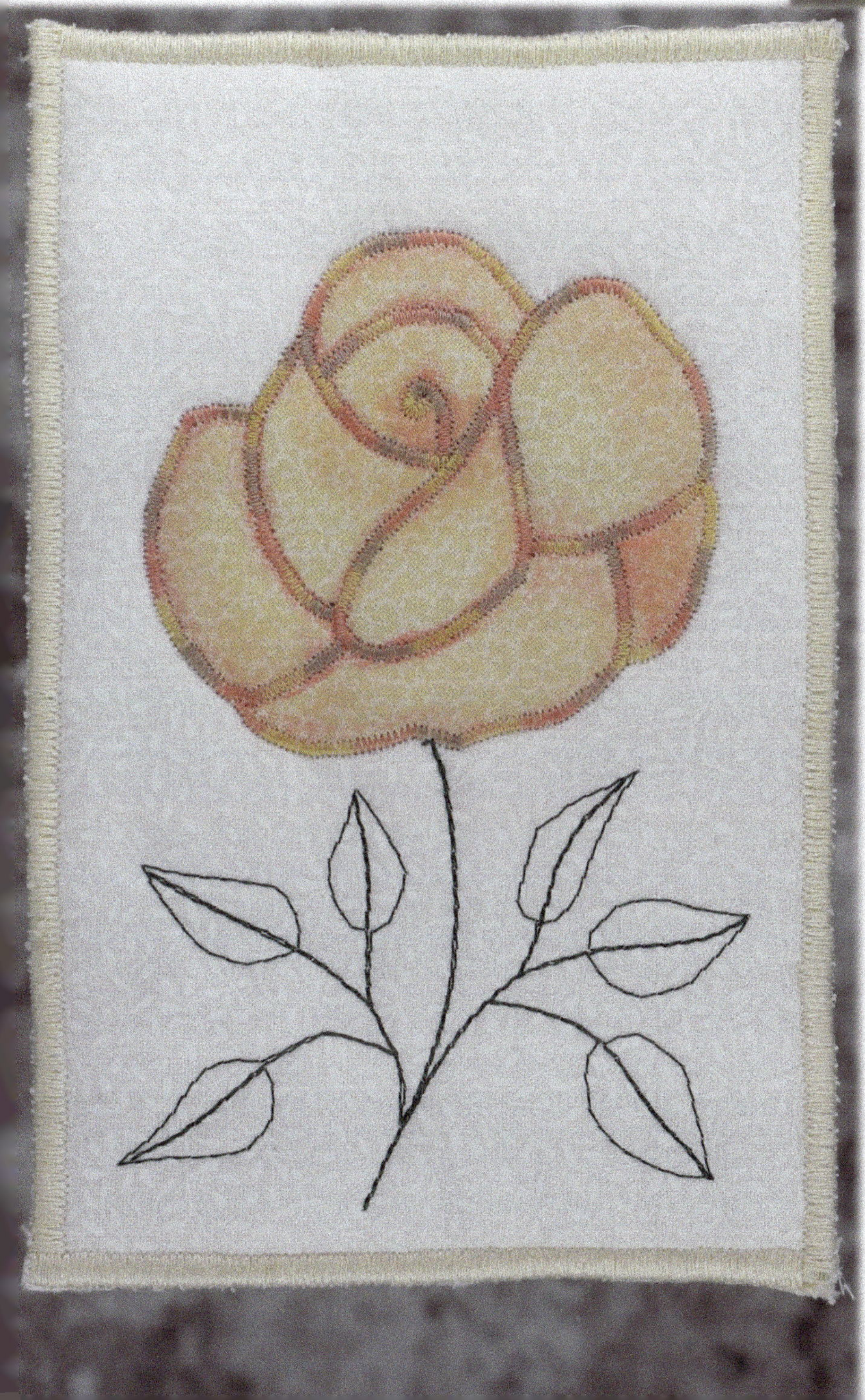

You will notice for the coaster I tend to use a zig zag stitch as I feel this is better for the usage that a coaster will get.

I have used Crayola crayons to add depth to the petals and stitched it in narrow zig zag stitch in a variegated thread. Rather than have fabric leaves I have just quilted them.

Sometimes when looking for the right fabric, the wrong side can be the right side!!! For this rose I used the wrong side of the fabric as it was paler and suited what I wanted to achieve. The edge of the petals are highlighted with crayons.

Template for Rose

Jacobean Flower

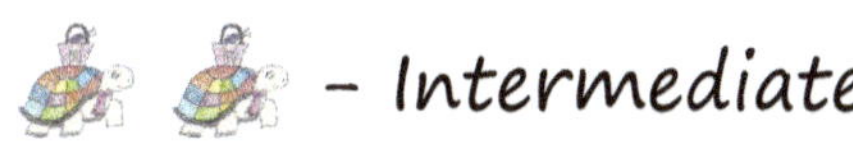 – Intermediate

I am fascinated by the history of certain patterns and designs, like Jacobean crewelwork. We tend to call these stylised designs Jacobean as this is when it became really popular (Jacobus is the Latin form of James e.g. King James I & VI) and we have a lot of surviving pieces and yet its designs are a lot older, going back to the Moors and Persia. Crewelwork embroidery is typically done with a fine worsted wool. But the designs in Jacobean crewelwork lend themselves to being sources for all different mediums, in this case fabrics.

You will need to make this postcard

2 pieces of white cotton fabric 4½" x 6½"

2 pieces of iron-on interfacing 4½" x 6½"

1 piece of wadding 4" x 6"

Fusible web

A selection of fabrics

A selection of threads

Stranded embroidery cotton in green and brown

1) Draw the sections of the flower onto the paper side of the fusible web and cut out with ¼" extra all round.

I have used a narrow zig zag for this design and the blue is a variegated thread.

2) Press onto the chosen fabrics and cut out on the line.

6) Draw on the stem, leaves and earth and then embroider them using two strands of embroidery cotton.

3) Press the design pieces onto the prepared background fabric.

For the stem I have used chain stitch and for the other bits stem stitch.

4) Layer with the wadding and rectangle of white fabric.

7) Pin the stabilised white fabric rectangle on the back and stitch around a number of times till you are happy with the finish.

5) Machine stitch the design.

With the variation I have added
more details in embroidery to the
design, with the trellis in the centre
of the flower and the piece up the
side of the petal.

Template for Jacobean Flower

Camellia

 – Intermediate

There are a lot of plants and flowers that I like but many I don't see often, only when we go to big gardens. The camellia is one of those. It comes in lots of different sizes, shapes and colours, both the plants and the flowers. It isn't a plant I would grow in my garden as I don't have the space.

You will need to make this postcard

2 pieces of white cotton fabric 4½" x 6½"

2 pieces of iron-on interfacing 4½" x 6½"

1 piece of wadding 4" x 6"

Fusible web

A selection of fabrics

A selection of threads

Stranded embroidery cotton

1) Draw the inner petals and then the outer flower and centre circle onto the paper side of the fusible web and cut out with ¼" extra all round.

2) Press onto the chosen fabrics and cut out on the line.

3) Press the pieces onto the prepared background.

4) Draw the petals onto the flower.

5) Layer with the wadding and rectangle of white fabric.

6) Machine stitch the design.

I have gone with a narrow zig zag and a variegated thread for stitching this design.

7) Embroider around the edge of the centre using two strands of embroidery cotton and French knots.

8) Pin the stabilised white fabric rectangle on the back and stitch around a number of times till you are happy with the finish.

With this postcard I have created it with one piece of fabric, then drawn on all the petals and used Crayola crayons to give the blush colouration to each petal and then stitched the petals with a variegated thread in straight stitch.

With this postcard I have used the dark
green to represent the foliage and the white
to give some depth. The edges of the petals
have been highlighted with crayons.

For this Coaster
the background
was one piece
and then the
inner petals and
centre put on. I
have used zig zag
for the centre
and inner petals
then straight
stitch for the outer
petals.

Bowl filler, finished
size 3" square. The
background is cut
to 3½" square and
then just the
middle of the
flower is
appliqued onto it.

Template for Camellia

Dog Rose

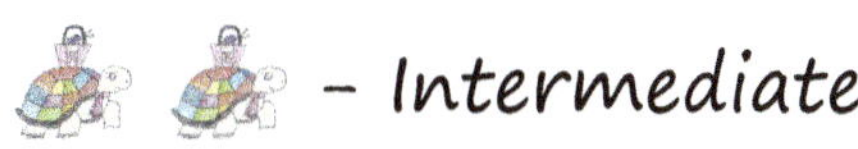 – Intermediate

This is the simplest rose, with five petals and is often seen in hedgerows, but it is also a bedding rose! The municipal park near us has planted a whole bed of dog roses and when in flower they are covered in tons of white/palest pink flowers and have a lovely scent. Then in autumn and winter there is the colour from the hips.

You will need to make this postcard

2 pieces of white cotton fabric 4½" x 6½"

2 pieces of iron-on interfacing 4½" x 6½"

1 piece of wadding 4" x 6"

Fusible web

A selection of fabrics

A selection of threads

Stranded embroidery cotton

1) Draw the whole flower, centre circle and twelve leaves onto the paper side of the fusible web and cut out with ¼" extra all round.

2) Press onto the chosen fabrics and cut out on the line.

3) Press the pieces onto the prepared background.

4) Draw the petals onto the flower.

5) Layer with the wadding and rectangle of white fabric.

6) Machine stitch the design.

I have chosen to use narrow zig zag for the centre and the petals in thread to match the colours and then I have gone with a dark green thread and straight stitch for all the leaves and stems.

7) Embroider around the edge of the centre using two strands of embroidery cotton and a combination of long straight stitches and French knots to create the stamens.

8) Pin the stabilised white fabric rectangle on the back and stitch around a number of times till you are happy with the finish.

I have used a white fabric to create the flower
and then coloured it in using different shades
of pink crayon, then stitched around using a
darker variated thread and straight stitch.

4" square coaster. I
have gone with pink
variegated thread
and a zig zag stitch.

Template for Dog Rose

Gerbera Daisy

 – Expert

Gerbera Daisies or any of the daisy family, including the small white ones - the Common Daisy that are considered weeds because they grow in lawns - are all cheerful flowers that bring a smile to my face. Of all the daisies it is the Gerbera that has been a big source of inspiration for Quilted Postcards and I have returned to them a number of times, making them in different colours and tweaking the design, as they can be bright and bold or soft and dreamy.

Just a warning!!! If you don't like doing French knots, then this postcard isn't for you. If you want to practice French knots then this postcard is brilliant for that. I love French knots and use them in so many of my postcards. There is something almost therapeutic about sitting quietly with my favourite music and stitching 100s of them!!!!

<table>
<tr><td>You will need to make this postcard</td><td>2 pieces of white cotton fabric 4½" x 6½"

2 pieces of iron-on interfacing 4½" x 6½"

1 piece of wadding 4" x 6"

Fusible web

A selection of fabrics

A selection of threads

Stranded embroidery cotton</td></tr>
</table>

This postcard is made a bit different. The only piece to be appliquéd on is the centre. The flower and background are all one piece of fabric.

1) The background and the design are the same piece of fabric. Prepare this first, as for a normal background by pressing the interfacing on the wrong side of the fabric and drawing the 4" x 6" rectangle on to it.

2) Draw the centre circle onto the paper
   side of the fusible web and cut out
   with ¼" extra all round.

3) Press onto the chosen fabric and cut
   out on the line.

4) Press the circle onto the centre of the
   prepared background fabric.

5) Make a card template of the petal
   and use this to draw the petals onto
   the fabric, going around the centre
   first then going out. Draw a swirl in the
   centre.

6) Layer with the wadding and rectangle
   of white fabric.

7) Machine stitch the design. Start by
   stitching, using standard straight stitch,
   the swirl in the centre and then round
   the edge of the centre. Then stitch the
   petals, starting in the middle and
   going round the first layer, then
   moving on to the outside ones.

8) Embroider around the edge of the centre using two strands of embroidery cotton and lots of French Knots.

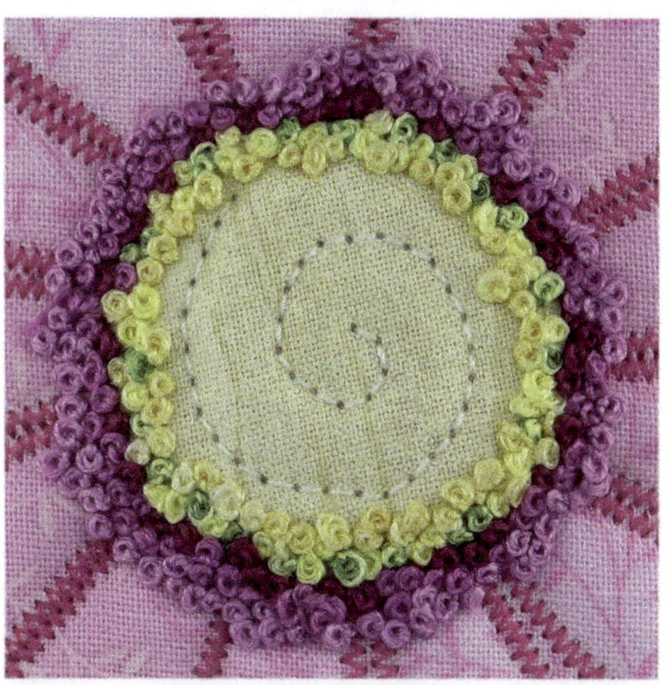

9) Pin the stabilised white fabric rectangle on the back and stitch around a number of times till you are happy with the finish.

Purple gerbera. With this one I have used a darker variegated thread and straight stitch. The centre is a dark colour and I have matched all the embroidery threads to the fabrics. It has created a darker moodier flower.

Yellow daisy. This one is just the inner petals, appliqued onto a background, with a brown centre.

Pink gerbera. With this one I have cut out the gerbera flower and attached it to a white background and stitched it in a thread that blends in with the fabric in a narrow zig zag. The centre stands out more.

This is the same fabric but just shows the difference you can create by using different colours of threads and techniques.

Template for Gerbera Daisy

Extra Template for Gerbera Daisy

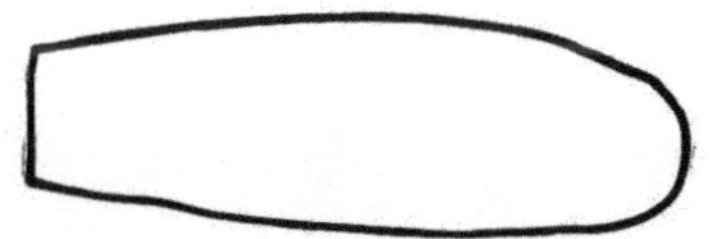

Hexagon Flower

 – Expert

To me, hexagons are the quintessential English patchwork, worked over papers for the perfect shape (EPP – English Paper Pieced!), they connect me back through history to all those women that sewed, for something to do or necessity. The first piece of patchwork I was taught was a hexagon, we made a pin cushion and its always the first thing I teach. I love hexagons and have made lots of different quilts using them, my favourite being the 'Grandmother Flower Garden' type.

So, when creating this book with a floral theme, a hexagon 'flower' just had to be included.

> **You will need to make this postcard**

> 2 pieces of white cotton fabric 4½" x 6½"
>
> 2 pieces of iron-on interfacing 4½" x 6½"
>
> 1 piece of wadding 4" x 6"
>
> Printer Paper
>
> A selection of fabrics
>
> A selection of sewing threads
>
> Yellow Stranded Embroidery Cotton

1) Make a copy of both the templates or use plastic templates if you have them.

2) Using the paper template or smaller plastic template, draw seven hexagons onto the paper and cut out.

When giving the measurements of hexagon templates, I always quote the side length. In this case the smaller paper one is a ½" and the bigger fabric one is ¾" side length.

3) Take the fabric template or larger plastic template and, on your chosen fabric, draw six hexagons for the petals and one for the centre.

4) Place a paper hexagon in the centre of the wrong side of the fabric hexagon and tack the fabric over the paper.

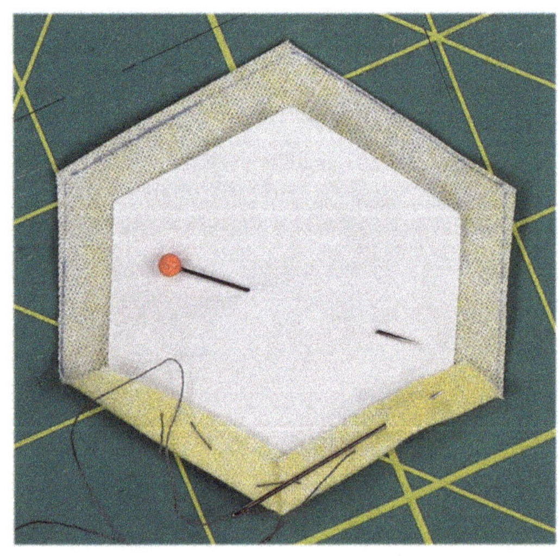

5) Stitch the hexagons together to make the flower.

6) Prepare the background.

7) Press the 'flower' and remove the tacking thread and papers. Pin centrally onto the prepared backing.

8) Slip stitch the hexagon 'flower' on to the background.

9) Mark on the leaves.

10) Layer with the wadding and rectangle of white fabric.

11) Quilt round the centre of the flower.

12) Machine stitch round the flower (on the background) and then the leaves.

13) Pin the stabilised white fabric rectangle onto the back and stitch round a number of times.

4" square Coaster with hexagon flower, random stitch embroidery in the centre and quilted leaves.

All of the hexagon flower items would make a lovely gift for a needlework friend, coaster, pin cushion and needle case all to match for their sewing space. Pattern for the needle case is on my website.

Bowl filler, finished size 3½" square. The background is cut to 4" square and the hexagon flower is appliqued on. The centre is embroidered and the leaves quilted.

Template Hexagon Flower

Template for Both Size Hexagons and Leaf

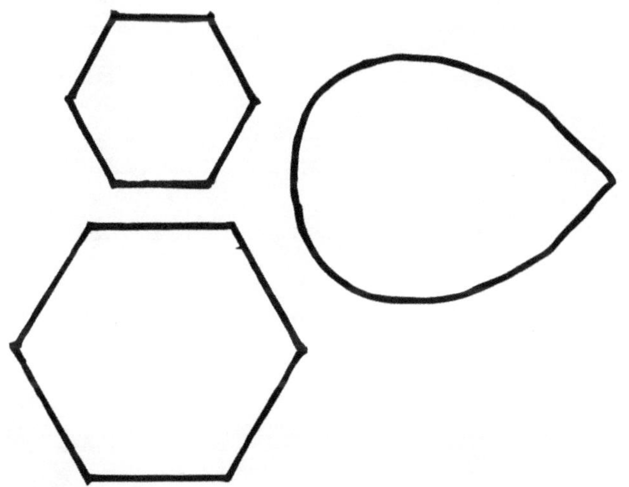

Nine Patch Flower

 – Expert

Nine Patch blocks are the fundamental starting design of so many traditional pieced blocks, and a design that is one of my favourites to create. They can create many designs.

One day, when looking at a cross stitch design of a very simple little flower, I saw them being created in fabric using the Nine Patch block and this postcard design was born.

1 square 1½" of yellow fabric for centre

4 squares 1½" of blue fabric for petals

4 squares 1½" of green fabric for leaves

2 pieces 1" x 3½" of green fabric

2 pieces 2" x 4½" of green fabric

2 pieces of white cotton fabric 4½" x 6½"

2 pieces of iron-on interfacing 4½" x 6½"

1 piece of wadding 4" x 6"

A selection of threads

1) Take the 1½" squares and lay out to form the Nine Patch flower design.

2) Stitch the squares together.

3) Press the stitched squares.

4) Take the 2 pieces 1" x 3½" and stitch
    to the top and bottom of the Nine
    Patch and press.

5) Take the 2 pieces 2" x 4½" and stitch
    them to each side of the Nine Patch
    and press.

6) Mark out the final size on the
    completed design.

7) Press a piece of interfacing onto the
    back.

8) Layer with the wadding and rectangle of white fabric.

9) Machine stitch the design.

Bowl filler or pin cushion. If using it as a pincushion it would look lovely with the decorative bee pins stuck in it!!

Finished size is 4" square and the centre is made from the nine 1½" squares, then 1" wide strips round the edges.

I stitched the design with straight stitch. I created a swirl in the yellow centre square to give texture, then I stitched curves in each of the blue squares to create petals and finally leaf shapes in the green corner squares. I stitched round the square and lines along the side panels.

10) Pin the stabilised white fabric rectangle on the back and stitch around a number of times till you are happy with the finish.

4" square Coasters. I have just machine quilted in straight stitch the circle in the centre, petals and leaves.

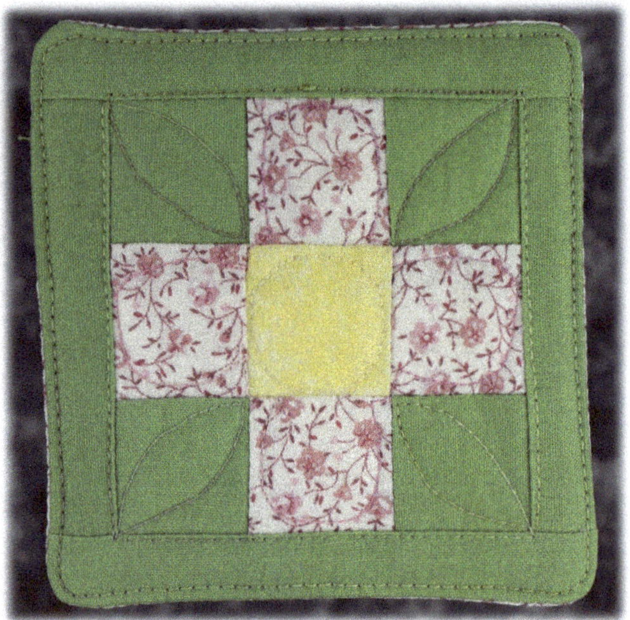

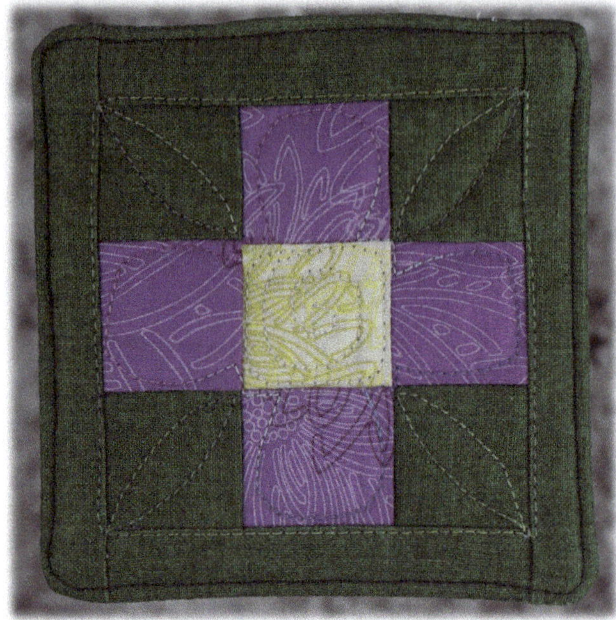

This is the same design but rather than the simpler machine quilting of the design, it has been embroidered. The centre has French knots and seed stitch. Seed stitch is just random small stitches. Then the petals are created with chain stitch and the leaves with straight line quilting all in two strands of stranded cotton embroidery thread.

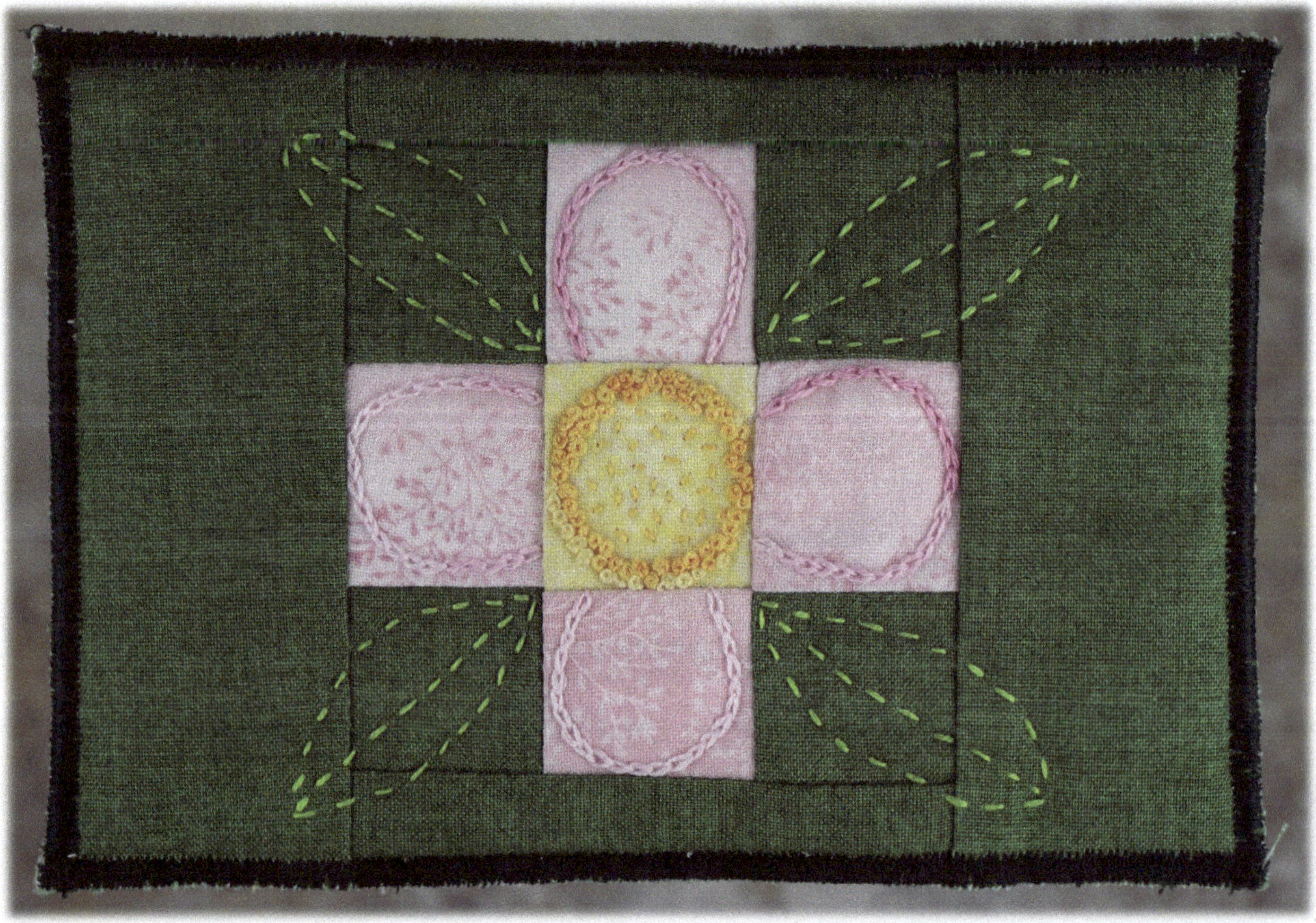

Template for Nine Patch Flower

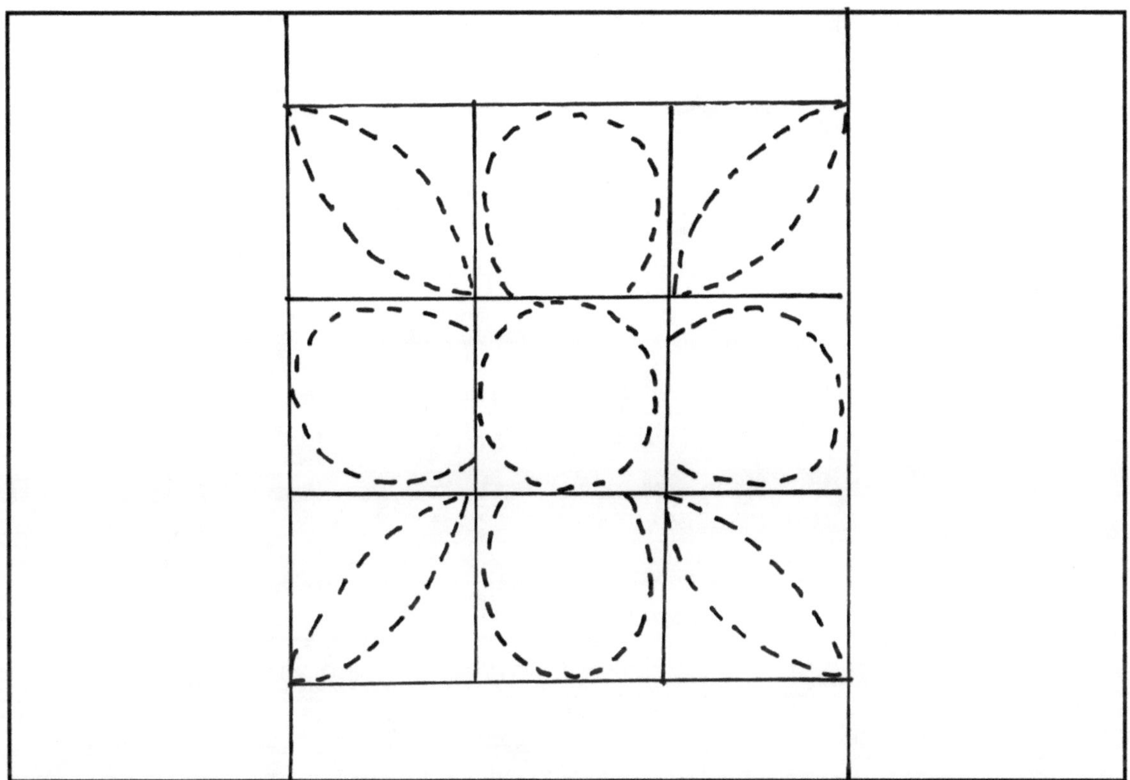

Crayon Coloured Flower

 – Expert

This is inspired by colouring books and being a child! Big bold shapes with black outlines and a box of crayons. I loved colouring in as a child and I still do as an adult! I can remember in junior school being told I had a good sense of colour and being asked by the girl sitting next to me if I could choose the colours for her picture as she really liked mine!

So, how did I end up using crayons on Quilted Postcards? I saw an article in an American Quilting magazine on using crayons to colour on quilts and since we had lots of crayons in the house - as Laura was young - I gave it a go!!! The method used was to melt the crayons and then 'paint' them onto the fabric. This got me thinking about actually colouring in with crayons and how this would work on fabric, which lead me to experimenting. And then, when I started making postcards, the two came together...

> **You will need to make this postcard**

> 3 pieces of white cotton fabric 4½" x 6½"
>
> 2 pieces of iron-on interfacing 4½" x 6½"
>
> 1 piece of wadding 4" x 6"
>
> Pigma Micron Pen in black
>
> Crayola crayons
>
> Kitchen Paper towel
>
> Embroidery cotton in yellow and pale Spring green
>
> Black or very dark grey sewing thread

One thing I learnt very early on when 'playing' with crayons, be it melting to paint on or colouring on, that a good quality crayon, which melts well and has a good pigment is best – for me this is Crayola Crayons. I recommend starting with a simple box of 24, then you can buy a bigger pack with more colours if you enjoy using them.

1) Take one piece of the white cotton and press a piece of interfacing onto the back, this will be the background of the postcard.

2) Place the background, fabric side up on top of the Design Sheet and using the Pigma Micron pen draw the design onto the fabric.

3) Start by colouring the centre of the main flower in with a yellow.

4) Go to your ironing mat, cover the postcard with the paper towel and press with a hot dry iron. Leave the iron sitting on the work for a few minutes to really heat the crayon and melt it into the fabric.

5) Let the postcard cool and then add more colour, building up the shades slowly. Press between each application of crayon.

6) Colour in all the flowers. Give the postcard a final good press to melt everything in.

7) Layer with the wadding and rectangle of white fabric.

8) Machine stitch the design on the black lines.

9) Embroider the centre of the flowers using a combination of French knots and seed stitch.

9) Pin the stabilised white fabric rectangle on the back and stitch round a number of times.

This postcard is quilted using
a black thread for the
outlines as the stronger
colours work better with a
black. I have used a bright
coordinating thread for the
edges.

These postcards are stitched with
a very dark grey as they are lighter
but the edges are done in
different coordinating colours
which changes the look again.

This is just a single flower and the whole postcard coloured, both the flower and the background.

This is the same design but the whole thing coloured in with crayon, all the flowers and the background.

Template for Crayon Coloured Flower

Throughout this book I have used crayons to colour in on a lot of the variations of the designs. I have used them to add depth and texture to the flowers and they are all worked in the same way – colouring in and melting with a hot dry iron, building the shades up slowly, as you would with coloured pencils on paper. With a lot of my Quilted Postcards, especially the floral ones but also the landscape ones and my journal quilts I use crayons. I don't use them on quilts or other bits that will get well used and washed as I find that, unless very carefully hand washed in a cold wash, they will fade and wash away. But for the 'art' stuff I do they are a great way to add colour, a lot better than fabric pens or paints (well, in my opinion and I have tried a lot of them!!!).

Bowl Fillers

Decorative small items that really have no function but to look pretty in a bowl!!!

Otherwise known as pin cushions or mini cushions!!

I came across fabric/patchwork bowl fillers a couple of years ago, the ones I saw were wool applique and I thought I can do similar in cotton fabrics. And I have since made loads, to display them all I would need a very big bowl – more a basket!!! I have a changing selection in a bowl and I also use them with Quilted Postcards, mini pictures, hoop art and other bits on my mantel shelf, this display changes every month to a different theme.

Other than being used just for decoration, they could be pin cushions or if a few drops of essence oils added to them as scented drawer sachets, they would make a lovely gift.

What you need to make a bowl filler will vary depending on the design, but in general it will be something like this.

- Cotton fabric
- Iron-on interfacing
- Wadding
- Embroidery cotton
- Sewing thread
- Toy Filling

1) Take the background fabric and stitch on the borders if the bowl filler has them.

2) Press a piece of iron-on interfacing onto the back.

3) Mark the design on the fusible web, cut out, press onto the wrong side of the fabric and cut out on the marked line.

4) Press the design onto the prepared background.

5) Layer with waddings and cotton fabric, stitch and embroider.

6) Tack round the edges, 1/8" in from the edge, trim off any excess wadding and fabric.

7) Cut a piece of fabric the same size as the front, and pin the front, right sides together, to it.

8) Stitch together, using ¼" seam allowance. Remember to leave an opening for turning.

9) Turn the right way round and stuff.

10) Slip stitch the opening closed and enjoy your bowl filler!!!

Coaster

Who doesn't need a coaster to put your favourite mug of coffee, tea or hot chocolate on? (Or even a G&T!!!)

As an alternative to making a Quilted Postcard as a gift/card I have on a few occasions made a coaster and attached this to a card instead. I always write a little note on the back saying about this being a coaster, so detach from the card and use.

Or you can make a whole set of them....

Cotton fabric

Iron-on interfacing

Wadding

Embroidery cotton

sewing thread

1) Cut the background 4½" square and press a piece of iron-on interfacing onto the back of the fabric.

2) Make up the design in the same way as for the Quilted Postcard and layer with wadding and cotton fabric before stitching and embroidering.

3) Tack round the edge, 1/8" in from the edge.

4) Trim off any excess wadding and fabric.

5) Cut a piece of fabric 4½" square for the back. Pin both pieces right side together.

6) Stitch round using ¼" seam allowance remembering to leave an opening for turning.

7) Trim the corners and turn the right way.

8) Press well.

9) Stitch 1/8" from the edge, through all the layers, this just finishes it off and also sews shut where it was open for turning. Remember to pull the threads to the back, knot off and then pull through the fabric.

Embroidery Stitches

I mainly use three proper embroidery stitches, for the details. I do also use random different length stitches for things like grass or to add texture. I have given basic instructions for Split Stitch, French knot and Lazy Daisy stitch but like everything else in this book, it is only what I use, please use whatever stitches you want to.

French Knot

1) Bring the threaded needle up where you want the French knot to be.

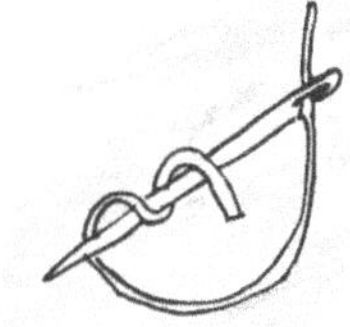

2) Hold the needle horizontal to the fabric and wrap the thread round the needle, two or three times, holding the thread taut.

3) Insert the needle through the fabric, right next to where it came out, keeping the thread taut and pull the needle through the fabric to form the knot.

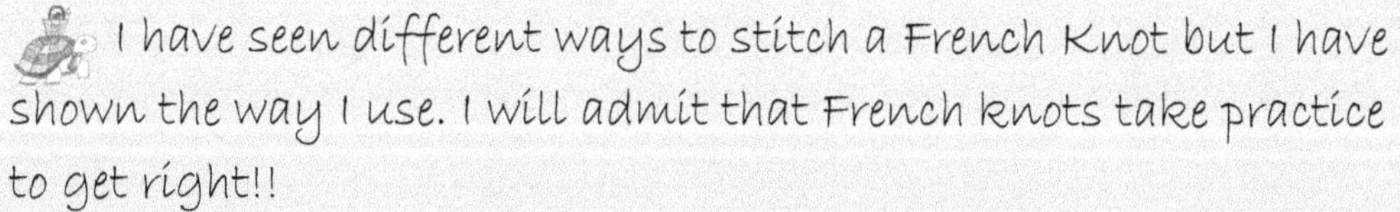

I have seen different ways to stitch a French Knot but I have shown the way I use. I will admit that French knots take practice to get right!!

The number of times I wrap the thread round the needle, depends on the look I am trying to get, twice round creates a smaller knot, three times a bigger one. By holding the thread taut as I pull the needle through gives a tight knot, if you want a baggier knot don't hold it taut. And finally I don't go back down the hole the thread comes out, as it is more likely for the knot to disappear and slip to the back!!! I insert the needle just next to it.

Split Stitch

1) Bring the threaded needle up to the front of the fabric at the start of the line to be stitched and create one basic stitch.

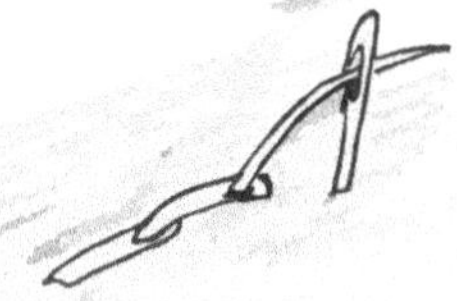

2) Then bring the needle back through to the front of the fabric a third of the way down the first stitch, 'splitting' the thread.

3) Take the needle to the back of the fabric to finish the stitch. Continue creating stitches in this way.

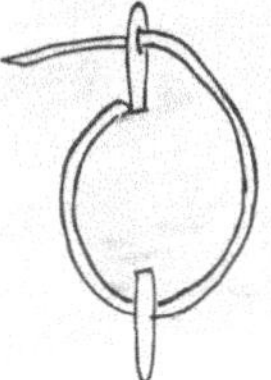

> I prefer the look of this stitch rather than the more common Back Stitch. The other stitch that is similar in look to Split Stitch is Stem Stitch
>
> By changing the length of your stitch you can create a smooth line, so going round curves or circles I will use smaller stitches than on a straight line.

Lazy Daisy Stitch (And Chain Stitch)

1) Bring the threaded needle up where you want the stitch to start. Take it back down right next to it, but don't pull the eye through.

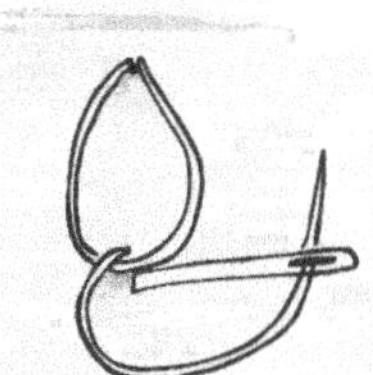

2) Bring the needle back up where you want the stitch to finish making sure the thread is sandwiched between the point of the needle and the fabric.

3) Pull the thread to form a loop.

4) Bring the needle down the other side of the thread, creating a small holding stitch.

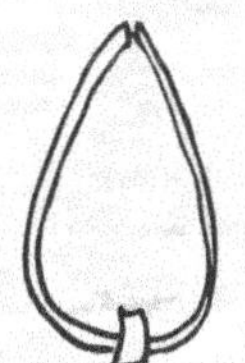

> Lazy Daisy Stitch is a single unit of Chain Stitch and is really good for flower petals.

About Me!

Since I was nineteen years old I have been creating patchwork quilts and other fabric items after I went to The National Patchwork Championship just to fill the coach that was going. I did go to classes to learn the basics of patchwork and quilting for two years but since then I am self-taught and have no formal qualifications in any art or design subject. My ethos on designing is not only for my own enjoyment but to make sure that they are able to be made by anyone with basic sewing skills. Quilts should not be scary. The Quilted Postcards are just part of the creativity that surrounds me. I have been teaching Patchwork and Quilting for a long time, in recent years at my local Arts Centre, and I have had work published in magazines.

I made my first Quilted Postcard in 2008. I saw an article on creating postcards with pre-printed fabric and at that time I was trying to find something to replace the ties I had been making for my husband Tony. For about 15 years I had been making mad, loud ties for Tony for birthdays, Christmases and any other time I wanted to give him a gift. He was known at his work for his ties (and yes he wore them everyday). Then the company decided that the engineers had to wear logo-ed polo shirts and I no longer had something to make for him.

The idea of Quilted Postcards really appealed to me and so I began creating them – first of all using the designs from the ties – just for Tony. Then our daughter Laura decided she liked them and from there it has spread to family and friends. I normally make around 100 a year for various friends and family as well as just to make for myself. I make them for birthdays, Christmases, Easter, and just as a personal gift. Or, if you are Laura, one 'Yellow Duck' postcard a month until she turned 18 and I ran out of ideas, although she did get 21 ducks on a quilt for her 21st.

One of my dreams has always been to write a book. After many years talking about it, starting and stopping multiple times, and with a lot of nagging from Tony and Laura we created the first book – 'Quilted Postcards – Little Quilts of Creativity' – in 2020. This is the second book dedicated to the abundance of floral inspired postcards within my collection. We have barely even scratched the surface on all my designs so keep an eye out for more.

The Tortoise Logo

As a child on holiday in Yorkshire, I can remember going to a museum/workshop of a furniture maker. He carved a mouse into all his creations. That man was Robert Thompson. The idea of a having an animal on everything to identify it has always stayed with me.

When I was looking for a logo to 'stamp' on my postcards, using the tortoise just felt right. It had been a long running joke between Tony and I that I was happy to stay safely in my shell/home. I drew up my tortoise logo – no plain, normal shell but a patchwork of colours with a scarf – I do love scarves – and carrying a bag of knitting – something else I do, along with crochet and weaving. The tortoise is me.

The Scary Electronic Place aka. 'The Internet'

I find it brilliant for finding out information and falling down rabbit holes (not so sure the latter is necessarily a good thing as time disappears…). I regularly post on both Facebook and Instagram using the handle 'Tortoise Crafts', not only to showcase my designs and what I am working on, but also in the hope of inspiring others. It's not just about Quilted Postcards but every other piece of fabric and fibre art I do – from weaving, knitting and crochet, to embroidery, quilts, and postcards. In the past year Tortoise Crafts has expanded to be not just myself but also my daughter's embroideries. You can find me at *www.tortoisecrafts.co.uk* where I upload my 'Rambles' (my version of a blog post which meanders off topic quite impressively, hence the name) on a semi-regular basis whenever something inspires me.

Sarah

p.s. We also have an Etsy Store - www.etsy.com/uk/shop/TortoiseCrafts

Quilted Postcards—Little Quilts Of Creativity

My first book is available on Amazon or available to order from your local book shop.

"Fantastic […] the instructions are very clear and the photography is of a high quality […] I highly recommend it." – 5 stars

"Amazing […] so easy to follow […] it kept me busy for hours." – 5 stars

"Really good set of designs […] instructions are really clear." – 5 stars

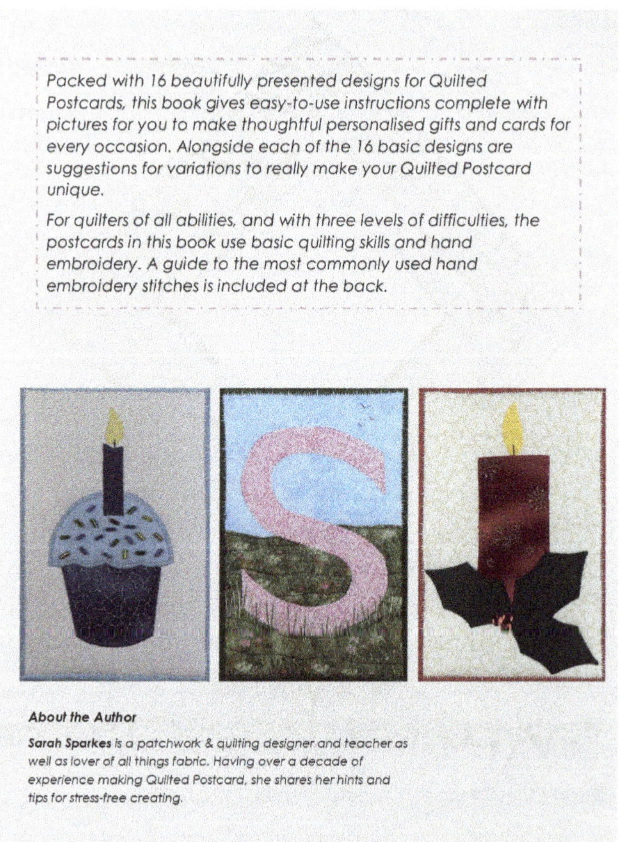

Social Media

You can find me on:

 www.tortoisecrafts.co.uk

www.facebook.com/tortoisecrafts/

www.instagram.com/tortoisecrafts/

www.youtube.com/channel/UCmNPRd2UIS5ClAM59qZusog